THE LANGUAGE OF SCHOOLING

Russell Dobson
Judith Dobson

UNIVERSITY
PRESS OF
AMERICA

Library of Congress Catalog Card Number: **81-40594**

To Mark, Mike, Susan

and Steve

ACKNOWLEDGEMENTS

In the preparation of this monograph, the authors are grateful to many people for their assistance. They are particularly indebted to the students in their classes at Oklahoma State University, whose cooperation made possible a thorough trial of this manuscript.

TABLE OF CONTENTS

PREFACE

Arriving at concensus relative to the purposes and functions of schooling requires responses to complex questions for which there are probably no best answers. Expressed purposes of schooling are as diversified and unique as the individual perceptual filters of those providing opinions.

The power of words (languaging) is probably the most overlooked, least understood, and ultimately neglected phenomenon in the field of education. Words serve to produce a paradoxical situation; both the freezing and unfreezing of reality. Unfortunately with the technical emphasis in the field of education on definition of terms along with the use of observeable behavior to explain the human condition they (words) tend to provide more of a freezing function.

Humans invented words to serve as a tool and now they are controlled by this tool. Language which was intended to explain or describe reality has become our reality. What we can't explain we tend to ignore and ultimately dismiss.

Indeed, if we are to pursue the roots of reality relative to the purposes of schooling we must uncover the meanings of words blurred by custom and usage. The crucial need is for "languaging" -- a way of discussing issues without arguing. Certainly, in a democracy with a pluralistic or multi-value base, there is a need for a communication vehicle that will assist persons in at least approaching concensus concerning the schooling of children. As responsible educators we can ill afford to leave the education of the young to the persuasive powers of a few.

This monograph enables persons interested in the purposes and functions of schooling to make useful distinctions among three explicit educational camps: Behaviorism, Experimentalism, and Humanism. Generally, the monograph provides a philosophical/theoretical base for each of the three camps and then explains what each approach may resemble in daily classroom practice.

Section I focuses on traditional educational issues, such as discipline, grading and minimal competencies. Section II presents a working definition of each of the three educational camps and should be read prior to the rest of the monograph. Section III presents an historical perspective, a theoretical definition, and operational examples of Behaviorism, education by Basic Design. Section IV attends to these same areas for Experimentalism, education by Developmental Design while Section V focuses on Humanism-Existentialism, or education by Natural Design.

Two thousand years ago the Stoic philosopher Epictetus wrote, "Men are disturbed not by things, but by the vision which they take of them." This monograph discusses varying views of what constitutes the purposes and practices of education.

Stillwater, Oklahoma   Russell Dobson
June, 1981   Judith Dobson

Section I

ROOTS OF CONFLICTING RHETORIC

Today's schools, like other public institutions, are a subject of concern to the taxpayer. The school is obligated to meet the educational needs of children, a task that has always been difficult and complicated, and is increasingly demanding today because of social, economic and political problems.

Some of the adult concerns in modern life that are being aggressively expressed toward practices in schools are:

> inflating costs of education,
>
> early and persistent anxiety of parents about their child's ability to be admitted to college,
>
> increasing importance placed upon vocation and citizenship training, and
>
> heightened regard for educational needs of special groups of children, such as the culturally different, learning disabled and intellectually talented.

Pressures for change that have resulted in controversy center around the following topics:

> theory - practice dilemma,
>
> the grading, marking, and reporting system,
>
> discipline,
>
> formal academic learning,
>
> ability grouping,
>
> student motivation,
>
> academic excellence or minimal competency,
>
> teacher performance (quality),

1

parent involvement, and

emphasis on the humanities, including the arts.

Educational decisions relative to these matters are being made all over the country. Innovative programs are being discarded, and new programs of "excellence" are being initiated. There exists the danger of embracing different methods, techniques and programs wholeheartedly and noncritically.

In a time when educators are overwhelmingly concerned with justifying what they are doing and citizens are eager to hold them accountable, is it not appropriate to attempt to make sense out of the controversy surrounding the purposes and function of the school? This section is committed to identifying the roots of conflicting rhetoric in the hope of facilitating responsible leaders as they appraise current schooling practices.

Ebel (1972) raises questions relative to the purpose of schooling. His first question is: "If the schools are to be accountable for the performance of their pupils, the question that immediately arises is, what performance (p. 3)?" He continues with a second query: "What should be the relative emphasis placed on affective dispositions as opposed to cognitive capabilities (p. 4)?"

Basic Questions

In an effort to resolve the issues, questions similar to the following need to be posed and seriously considered:

What constitutes a quality civilization?

What human or humane skills does one need in order to participate effectively in a quality civilization?

How do we want children to be different as a consequence of a schooling experience?

What kind of criteria are necessary for the realization of these goals?

What are the major social problems confronting contemporary society?

What might the schools have done to con-
tribute to these social problems?

What do I value? or What is important?

How does a human experience labeled
schooling make a difference?

These are complex questions for which there probably is no one or best answer. No doubt, responses
provide individuals with their own answers to the
broader question, "What are the basics?" However,
gaining concensus among individuals is quite another
matter.

Critical Issues

Theory-Practice Dilemma. As teachers have increased their militance, professors of education have
lost credibility with their constituents. An anti-
theoretical bias seems to be prevalent among many
teachers. College classes are seen as irrelevant and
not related to the day to day operations of the classroom. On the other hand, professors are frustrated by
the lack of attention given to theory in decision-
making at the public school level. In an age of inex-
haustible ideas the temptation has been to adopt new
ideas indiscriminately and apply them inappropriately.
With only a superficial understanding of the basic
theories on which innovations are based, we tend to
implement them unwisely, and when they do not yield
the expected results we reject the innovations as
hastily as we accepted them.

Grading, Marking, and Reporting System. Those
who believe that grading is a minor problem are simply
not cognizant of what is happening in the schools.
Grading, marking and reporting determine more
teaching-learning situations than most people imagine.
Students from kindergarten through graduate school
realize that grading dominates most of their learning.
Teachers, counselors and school administrators grapple
with parents about the fairness of grades. Whenever
and wherever teaching and learning occur, grades or
grading procedure are a grim reality for most people.

3

Current grading practices are viewed by some as a primitive system which categorizes participants so that only a few are successful. The source of the categorization scheme is the normal curve. The normal curve distribution is most appropriate to chance and random activity and therefore, is definitely not sacred (Bloom 1968; Van Hoven, 1972; Bailey, 1975; Evans, 1976; Bellanca and Kirschenbaum, 1976; Simon, 1977).

The apparent discrepancy existing among various camps concerning grades centers around accepted truths about grading. Curwin (1976, p. 38) identifies four of these considered truths: "(1) learning requires evaluation, (2) grades are motivators, (3) grades are, or can be, objective, and (4) grades are needed as a screening device for colleges, graduate schools, and employers." These four points are sources of disagreement as far as grading and evaluation are concerned and must be dealt with in attempts to resolve the grading dilemma.

Discipline. Today, behavior problems of children are a subject of increasing concern and interest. The attitudes of parents, teachers, counselors, lay public, and school administrators toward the disciplining of pupils have received critical examination during the past decade as the result of two separate, but closely related factors: (1) the current attacks on public schools, and (2) the highly publicized examples of juvenile delinquency. Success and failure of teachers are frequently reported in terms of pupil control. The maintenance of order and discipline in the classroom is often rated at the top of the list of problems teachers consider as their major difficulties.

Although there is wide variations in the interpretation of what constitutes adequate discipline in the classroom and how to attain it, there seems to be near uniformity of opinion that unless teachers and pupils work together in harmony toward desired ends, little of value can be accomplished.

Academic Excellence and/or Minimal Competency. Increasingly, educators are finding themselves involved in the minimal competency movement (Farr and Olshavsky, 1980; Pipho, 1978; Turlington, 1979). Several states have determined that students must meet statewide reading, writing, and arithmetic standards before promotion or graduation.

4

Much of the lay public, and an increasing number of educators, see the job of the school as quite simply—to help pupils learn. Priority, they say, should be assigned to cultivation of cognitive competence. Basic hard-liners, according to Brodinsky (1977, p. 524), are proposing simplistic demands for the so-called 3 R's with ". . . (1) minimal competency, (2) proficiency testing, and (3) a performance-based curriculum."

On the other hand, moderates or liberals, depending on one's preferential label, are somewhat skeptical of what they see as a limited view of schooling. Rogers and Baron (1976, p. 311) point to changes in American life style that have an affect on the academic performance of students.

Opponents to the hard core academic excellence movement are not opposed to teaching basics, but rather question a limited perspective of what constitutes basics. They see academic excellence as incorporating, along with the 3 R's, the ability to think, analyze problems, make wise decisions, and develop confidence in self. They opt for an expanded view of basics: the development of life skills, that lead to the competencies needed for personal growth, for successful existence as a citizen, consumer, job holder, taxpayer, and a member of a family.

What was excellence yesterday may not constitute excellence today nor be considered excellence in 10 or 15 years. Educators must begin diligently to examine and discuss the meaning of academic excellence.

Ability Grouping. The issues involving homogeneous grouping frequently are reduced to the question of whether or not to practice "ability" grouping. Homogeneous grouping is a practice wherein the total student population is divided into instructional groups according to some criterion of likeness. The basic premise in class assignment by ability grouping is the belief that learning is facilitated when children of similar abilities or academic achievement are together for instruction.

Advocates of homogeneous grouping are vociferous in expounding the merits of this arrangement. Strengths proclaimed by proponents are: (1) special attention may be paid to children's abilities or talents; (2) superior academic achievement may be attained; (3) materials and procedures may be adapted more easily; and (4) administrative procedures may be facilitated.

Opponents of ability grouping argue that: (1) children are usually typed and placed at one level permanently; (2) the organizational patterns may become a rigid administrative pattern; (3) a balanced curriculum is difficult to maintain; (4) segregation of children is inconsistent with democratic values; (5) teachers are encouraged to believe that children are alike; and (6) stimulation by peers of various abilities and talents is lacking (Daniels, 1961; Rosenthal and Jacobson, 1968; Johnson and Johnson, 1975).

Student Motivation. Controversy surrounding student motivation is centered around the argument of intrinsic and extrinsic rewards. Some educators submit that adults, because of life experience, know better than children what the children should be when they grow up. The task of teachers is to determine strategies for getting children to do what they should do. In order to achieve this goal, teachers establish a system of positive reinforcement.

Opponents of this approach to student motivation do not deny that positive reinforcement is more satisfying than negative reinforcement. However, they argue that both are externally directed. They fear that over an extended period of time children will reach the point where they perform only when an incentive is available. They further submit that if educators are committed to the notion of the self-directed learner then placing an excessive amount of value on behavior modification techniques may delay unnecessarily, if not permanently, learners' acceptance of responsibility for their own learning (Deci, 1972a, 1972b; Garbarino, 1975; Lepper and Green, 1976).

Quality Teachers. Negative postures relative to the quality of teachers is presently being assumed by many concerned persons. Advocates of this position seem to assume that good teaching is basically a matter of determination and discipline. According to Frazier (1976) such individuals believe:

1. Teachers will teach better when they themselves are better taught. Competency is

the key, performance the proof. New
teaching know-how can and will do the
trick.

2. When we learn how to separate the can-do's
from the no-can-do's among candidates for
certification, we will get better teaching.

3. Let's do away with tenure. With the fear
of dismissal always before them, teachers
will buckle down to business. Get results
or out you go (p. 138).

The rationale of those educators taking opposi-
tion to this point of view is that teacher preparation, certification standards, and supervision have
never been better than they are at the present time.
They argue that the need is to release rather than
restrain teacher energy.

Parental and Community Involvement. Currently,
community residents and parents are demanding an
active voice in extremely sensitive areas of educational decision-making that within the past 70 years
were solely delegated to boards of education and
school administrators. If public schools are to
regain the credibility once assigned to them by the
public, then means of involvement and open communication with the schools' clientele must be established
(Dobson and Dobson, 1975).

Educators must mount new efforts to demonstrate,
with integrity, that the schools are indeed public.
Progressive educators are already involved in designing ways to involve parents and community as partners
in the school's functions. Advisory groups, decentra-
lization, and employement of para-professionals are
but a few of the current trends being utilized to establish open communication (Dobson and Dobson, 1981).

Summary

An anonymous sage once said, "The cause of any-
thing is everything." This proposition embodies the
notion of the interrelatedness of all things. Today
the search goes on for the purposes of schooling. The
purposes no doubt are varied and interrelated but the
more fundamental are resultant of attempts to answer

two basic questions put forth by MacDonald (1977): (1) What is the meaning of life? and (2) How can we work together?

It should come as no surprise that in a troubled society some would seek a national solution in "returning to basics." Let us recapitulate. There is a progressively widening split in the ranks of persons concerned with pruposes of the school experience in the United States, a split that has resulted in definite trends in both theory and practice.

Although many educational issues are raised in the debate, they can be categorized under one of two broad headings, either (1) discipline, or (2) academic excellence. For many years our society has been concerned with how children behave and what and how much they are learning in school.

SCHOOL LANGUAGE

Being critical of the nation's schools has moved from a hobby stage to a full-blown national sport. Currently, demands are being made of schools from pressure groups involved in the so-called "Back to Basics" movement.

Deciding on the purposes of schooling results in complex questions for which there probably are no best answers. Nevertheless, these questions must not be set aside for the exclusive pondering of futuristic scientists and philosophers, but rather are questions that honestly must be confronted in a serious manner by all those involved, in whatever remote fashion, in the growth experiences of children.

Educational opinion, due to the uniqueness of individual perceptual filters, is contaminated with conventional wisdom; perspective without validity. We share a <u>Model</u> <u>for</u> <u>Education</u> <u>Dialogue</u> dialectically as we share the rest of the manuscript and its substance. The content of the model is presented for contemplation and discussion purposes only and is not intended to be final in nature. We feel obliged to remind readers that classification schemes are used to assist individuals in organizing their own perceptions of reality and not to express any notions of "absolute" reality. However, collective perceptions expressed as beliefs ultimately result in defined philosophic positions. Put another way, probably no individual or institution exists in "pure form" as far as the identifying characteristics of a particular "camp." But, as educators constantly entertain pressure and criticism it is useful for them to have classification tools for categorizing various education opinions.

The Model is our attempt to identify and contrast philosophical-psychological profiles that tend to separate into three camps: (1) Design A, (2) Design B, and (3) Design C. This separation is quite possibly a direct reflection of whether educators are primarily concerned with doing <u>to</u>, <u>for</u>, or <u>with</u> children.

A MODEL FOR EDUCATION DIALOGUE

BELIEFS	DESIGN A	DESIGN B	DESIGN C
	Movement Toward External Control		Movement Toward Internal Control

←——————————————————————————————————→

PHILOSOPHY

	DESIGN A	DESIGN B	DESIGN C
Nature of Humans	Humans are potentially evil.	Humans are potentially both good and bad or blank slate.	Human potential is basically good.
Nature of Learning	Truth exists separate from the individual. There are basic facts that are necessary for all. Learning occurs by reaction.	Truth is relative and subject to conditions of the learner and the environment. Learning occurs by action.	Truth is an individual matter. Learning occurs when the information encountered takes on personal meaning for the learner. Learning occurs by transaction and interaction.
Nature of Knowledge	Logical structure. Information. Subject matter. Vertical relationships. Universal.	Psychological structure. Vertical and horizontal relationships and interrelationships.	Perceptual structure. Relationships and interrelationships. Personal. Gestalt.
Nature of Society	Closed. Ordered. Institutionalized. Static. Grouping.	Influx. Democractic. Relative values. Experimentation.	Open. Self renewing. Individual. Liberating. Distribution. Egalitarian
Purpose of Education	To understand and apply knowledge. To control the environment. To learn absolute truth.	To learn prerequisite skills for survival. To learn conditional truths.	To live a full life. To experience the environment. To continue learning personal truth.

PSYCHOLOGY

Human Growth and Development	Growth is environmentally determined.	Growth is the realization of one's potential.	Growth is the celebration of one's potential.
Concept of Self	Determined by what others think. Focuses on personality deficiencies.	Determined by how the individual perceives the social environment (becoming-future orientation).	Determined and created by each individually (being-now orientation).
Human Emotions	Controlled. Closed. Unaware. Masked.	Circumstantial. Based on position. Well-adjusted.	Free. Openness. Spontaneity. Aware. Transparency. Experienced. Authentic.
Interpersonal Interactions	Role playing. Manipulative games. Defensive. Detached. Distrusting. Dependent.	Minimum risk. Selective. Objective. Exclusive. Encountering. Independent.	Sharing. Risking. Trusting. Nonpossessive. Mutual accessibility.

DAILY PRACTICES

Curriculum	Predetermined. Structured series. Logical sequence. Content centered. Outcomes established.	Sequenced experiences. Problem-centered. Future utility. Universalism.	Hidden. Unfolding. Created. Process centered. Unlimited. Emerging. Dynamic.
Instructional Behavior	Transmission of facts and content. Purposeful. Management. Teacher directed.	Grouping for instructional convenience. Inquiring. Discovering. Open questions with multiple answers. Teacher invitation.	Learner directed. Learner invitation. Teacher functions as source of safety and support.

11

Oganization	Established. Emphasis on management. Focus on homogeneous grouping.	Orchestration. Focus on skill grouping.	Changing circumstantial. Adaptive. Focus on heterogeneous grouping.
Evaluation Techniques	Measurement of facts and content. Determined by authority. Imposed. Product oriented.	Critical thinking. Problem solving. Tests higher cognitive skills. Focuses on what is learned.	Feedback by invitation. Cooperative pupil and teacher evaluation. Non-damaging comparison. Multiple techniques. Focuses on how one feels about what is learned as well as what is learned.

DEFINITION

Definitions of Curriculum	A structured series of intended learning outcomes. M. Johnson (1967)	A sequence of potential experiences set up in school for the purpose of disciplining children and youth in group ways of thinking and acting. Smith, Stanley, Shores (1957)	An attempted definition of humans translated into educational specifications. R. Dobson
Representative Language	Structure. Management. Reinforcement. Shaping. Labeling. Performance. Accountability. Objectives. Behavior. Matching. Environment. Cause-effect. Measurement. Observation. Transmission of roles and functions. Control. Intelligence. Reality. Order. Standards. Tests. Grades. Cover. Direct.	Sequence. Stages. Growth and development. Becoming. Correlated. Interest. Programs. Diagnostic. Readiness. Technique. Skills. Activity. Individual differences. Rational. Well-adjusted. Motivation. Progress. Expectations. Understanding. Discipline. Knowledge. Evaluate. Enable. Support. Facilitate. Guide. Help. Meaningful.	Being. Desires. Process. Democratic. Freedom. Feedback. Fulfillment. Experience. Diversity. Perception. Potential. Harmony. Personal order. Self-direction. Accepting. Unique. Consequence. Potential. Awareness. Sharing. Trusting. Allow. Experiment. Involve. Issues. Options. Natural. Spontaneous. Personal meaning.

The three camps can be dispersed on a continuum ranging from training to education.*

Training (To)	(For)	Education (With)
(Essentialism-Behaviorism)	(Experimentalism-Cognitivism)	(Existentialism-Humanism)

According to MacDonald (1968), training is the process of preparing a person to perform defined functions in predictable situations, and education is the process of equipping an individual to perform undefined functions in unpredictable situations. An educational program committed to the training end of the continuum is based on the notion that children are the sum total of their experiences--passive victims of their environments. Conversely, the opposite end of the continuum is committed to the notion that children are active, goal-seeking organisms eager to profit from or celebrate encounters with their environments.

The basic beliefs applied to each of the three distinct educational camps are categorized into four parts (1) philosophy, (2) psychology, (3) daily practices, and (4) definitions.

The remainder of the manuscript is an in-depth exploration of the philosophical/psychological base of each of the three camps, and the translation of each base into day-to-day practice in the shool. Section III is devoted to Design A, Section IV is an analysis of Design B, and finally Section V is a discussion of Design C.

---

*For a more extensive discussion relative to this point the reader is referred to Chapter VI in Dobson and Dobson, Humaneness in the Schools: A Neglected Force, (Dubuque, Iowa: Kendall/Hunt Publishers, 1976).

Section III

DESIGN A

Curriculum development according to Design A is psychologically couched in Behaviorism and philosophically based in Essentialism. Behavioristic investigation is limited to objective, observable phenomena, and to the methods of natural science. Essentialism, a philosophical position, mediates between the Realist and Idealist extremes. Marshall (1973, p. 97) contends that Essentialists believe that ". . . some tradition must continue to be taught as the indisputable core of curriculum."

J. B. Watson, an American psychologist who leaned heavily upon the research of Pavlov, formulated Behaviorism around 1913. Watson proposed to make psychology scientific by utilizing only objective methods, including adaptations of Pavlov's conditioning techniques, investigations of human physiology, the study of animal behavior and laboratory experiments. Watson, who was an animal psychologist at John Hopkins University, objected to the concept of introspection, which he considered unscientific. He believed psychology's real concern was to study behavior, not consciousness.

At this same period in history, Edward L. Thorndike was formulating his theory of learning called S-R bond or connectionism. Thorndike (1912) assumed that through conditioning, specific responses come to be linked with specific stimuli. Thorndike's laws (1912, 1913, 1949) leave no room for insight and apparently do not require purposefulness of man nor of lower animals. It is Thorndike's name that is generally associated with the concept of trial and error (Bigge, 1964; Sargent and Stafford, 1965). Thorndike's works not only pervaded the development of the field of educational psychology but also were related in textbooks used by most teachers, counselors and school administrators. More specifically, Thorndike's research has had a tremendous impact upon current educational practices such as the popularization of standardized testing, accountability, and an emphasis upon teacher skills, strategies or techniques (Eisner, 1977).

The leading proponent of Behaviorism today is B. F. Skinner. Skinner conducted the first systematic

15

study of operant conditioning in 1938, and he and his associates have continually refined the process, referring to it as behavior shaping. According to Skinner, practically every detail of human behavior is shaped by reward and punishment in one form or another. Programmed learning is a relatively recent application of Skinner's operant conditioning/behavior shaping (Goldenson, 1975).

Sulzer and Mayer (1972, p. 2) emphasize that due to the influence of B. F. Skinner, there has been an increased interest in ". . . basic behavioral laboratory research as well as applied research in settings such as schools. . ." Their book is written on the basic assumption that what students do is of primary importance. They continue that behavioral change is implicit in any school program and that ". . . the decision is not whether behavior should be changed, but who will change it, what the goals will be, and which specific program of behavior change will be used." (p. 3).

Therefore, the teacher, counselor or school administrator adhering to the tenets of Behaviorism becomes a behavioral engineer (Dimick and Huff, 1970). The behavioral engineer, through the scientific application of empirically validated principles, not only brings about behavior modification in children but also manipulates environmental conditions so that the child can function optimally as defined by some outside authority.

The philosophical counterpart of Behaviorism is Essentialism which in American education is comprised of Idealism and Realism. Idealism as a school of thought began with Plato, often considered the Father of Idealism (Marler, 1975). The thinking of philosophers Descartes and Spinoza added to this particular philosophy. During our country's colonial period, Calvinist Johnathan Edward and Samuel Johnson emphasized the discipline of the mind as the instrument of gaining knowledge. During this same period, Immanuel Kant and George Hegel, among others, contributed to this particular school of thought. The man generally thought of as the Father of Modern Idealism is Bishop Berkeley.

Aristotle is considered the Father of Realism. However, John Locke, Johann Herbert, Alfred North Whitehead, Bertrand Russell and George Santayana are some of the notable contributors to this particular

16

philosophic thought. The Realism movement provided much of the philosophical basis for the school testing movement and the development of educational psychology. The intelligence scales of Binet and Terman and the measurement of curricular and instructional variables pursued by Thorndike and his successors have their roots in Realism.

The melding of Idealism and Realism extremes seems to produce Essentialism. Kneller (1964) identified four fundamental principles which provide the basis for the Essentialism movement. These are:

1. Learning involves hard work and often unwilling application. Emphasis is placed on the importance of discipline. The child attains personal control only through voluntary submission to discipline, imposed by the teacher.

2. The initiative in education lies with the teacher rather than the pupil.

3. Assimilation of prescribed subject matter is emphasized.

4. The school is obligated to retain traditional methods of mental discipline. Creative achievements of the past are sources of knowledge for dealing with problems of the present.

Therefore, teachers, counselors or school administrators who align themselves with the Essentialist philosophy believe that the purpose of education is both intellectual and moral discipline. The school has the role in society of ". . . preserving and transmitting the essential core of the culture and incidentally to the ordered evolutionary process of change" (Wingo, 1974, p. 620). The teacher, of course, is the active agent of this transmitting process.

Basic Beliefs: Are Your's Similar?

The Definition of Humans. Given this brief discussion of the underlying psychology of Design A, Behaviorism, and the philosophical basis of Essentialism, readers are encouraged to contemplate their agreement with the following assumptions:

1. Humans can be characterized clearly in terms of their behavior.

2. Humans are malleable and passive reactors to their environment which determines behavior.

3. The human is not free.

4. Good and bad behavior are determined by authority.

5. Human behavior is predictable.

6. Human characteristics can be studied independently of one another.

If you have inclined to agree with these assumptions then you are probably philosophically aligned with advocates of Design A. These persons believe that human potential tends toward evil. Therefore for the good of themselves and society children must be directed and controlled. These persons attempt to shape learners according to their values and teach them what they should know.

Motivation. Motivation is defined by Goldenson (1975, p. 536) as "the dynamics of behavior; the process of initiating, sustaining and directing the activities of the organism." Once again readers are urged to contemplate their degree of agreement with the following:

1. Behaviors which are reinforced (rewarded) are likely to recur.

2. Frequency of repetition is necessary in acquiring skills and in bringing about overlearning to guarantee retention.

3. Reinforcement (reward) must follow immediately after the desired behavior and be clearly connected with that behavior in the mind of the learner.

4. Appropriate external stimulation of the learner is necessary for optimal achievement.

If you agree with these assumptions then you are in accord with those who believe appropriate external

18

stimulation in the form of rewards or punishment is necessary for optimal achievement. Motivation is something to be done to someone.

Learning Conditions. Now, focus upon learning conditions, or your personal beliefs concerning essentials or requirements necessary for learning to take place. Consider your agreement with the following list of assumptions:

1. The human mind is an information receptacle which can produce factual content mastery.

2. Mastery of content is assisted by organization; therefore content presented to the learner should be ordered and systematic.

3. The mind consists of separate, but related faculties which can be trained.

4. Learning is largely a reactive experience.

5. Learning situations should be created to induce competition for rewards among learners.

People agreeing with these assumptions tend to see the mind as a giant psychological storehouse capable of receiving and holding a multitude of facts, concepts, and skills. When the occasion calls for one or more of these particles of learning to be recalled, the mind delivers it to the stage of action. The development of various skills through drill, practice, habit formation, and conditioning are all appropriate methods.

Social Learning. Social learning can be defined as the gradual acquisition of attitudes and behavior that enable the individual to function as a member of society. Inherent in this definition is the development of behavior patterns which are acceptable to society. Below is a list of assumptions which readers may wish to ponder as they attempt to delineate or to revisit beliefs concerning social learning.

1. Children do not know what is best for them and must be motivated to learn what is significant and contributory to their lives.

2. Adults, because of chronological age, know better than children what they should be when they grow up.

3. The purpose of school is to prepare children for adulthood so they can assume a contributing role in society.

4. Personality is a social product.

Those who suscribe to these assumptions emphasize the development of behavior patterns which are acceptable to society. Social learning is seen as the gradual acquisition of attitudes and behaviors that enable individuals to function as a member of society. Appropriate external stimulation usually in the form of rewards is necessary for optimal achievement.

Intellectual Development. Psychologists agree that intelligence is not a single entity, but a complex, multifacted set of abilities. Psychologist, however, disagree concerning whether or how much of intelligence is based upon innate capacity and how much is determined by environmental conditions.

Take a few moments to think about the following assumptions:

1. People possess different levels and amounts of intelligence. These levels can be ascertained and reported by a score derived from testing.

2. The normal curve expresses the social and academic expectation of where people are supposed to fit for the goodness of all.

If you tend to agree with these assumptions then you probably see intelligence as primarily a function of environmental conditions. In addition, you probably believe that persons possess different levels and amounts of intelligence.

Knowledge. Knowledge is certainly a prerequisite to enlightened citizenry. However, many school personnel have not clearly formulated in their own minds exactly what constitutes knowledge. Once again, take a risk and check yourself concerning your beliefs about the following assumptions:

20

1. Knowing is a process of reacting to stimulation.

2. Truth exists prior to the learning of it.

3. Truth can be known for itself and not merely for some instrumental purpose.

If you accept these assumptions then you probably agree with those who submit that a central body of knowledge exists that must be transmitted to all. The truth is pre-existent to the learning of it.

Society. The final list of assumptions in this section is presented below and deal with the concept of society:

1. The school preserves social order and builds new social orders when the public has decided they are needed.

2. Humans are made human by cultural birth.

According to persons suscribing to Design A, school is one of the most important institutions in society whose purpose is preservation of the culture. The school is the tool for maintaining existing social order and helping to build new social order when the authorities have decided. The task of the school is one of developing a standardized citizen as a product.

Did you generally agree or disagree with the assumptions stated in this section? We are not suggesting that beliefs can be neatly assigned in pure form to this or that camp, but that beliefs have a tendency to lean in certain directions. As you respond to the assumptions in Sections IV and V your philosophical profile should begin to be revealed. If no philosophical direction is revealed we recommend extensive study and introspection on your part. Educators make daily decisions that affect the lives of boys and girls; these decisions require a crystal clear theoretical/philosophical base. The remainder of this section attempts to translate the philosophical/psychological assumptions of Design A into daily classroom operations according to: (1) instruction, (2) curriculum, (3) organization, (4) resources, (5) physical space, and (6) evaluation.

21

Educational Practices

Instruction. Teachers who adhere to Design A believe that human potential tends toward evil. Therefore, children must be directed and controlled. This negative belief of man is often cloaked in expressions of restrained warmth as youngsters are manipulated toward predetermined goals. Therefore, the teacher masks, plays a role, or sets up games in order to maintain the status quo.

Since things are valued over people, rules and maintaining the status quo of the school take priority over children's needs, wants, and desires. Student production is valued and the child who does not produce that which is required at a predetermined level of competency is not a "good" student or is at best disabled.

The basic beliefs concerning human growth and development are centered upon humans as reactors to their environments. Therefore, children are the sum total of their experiences, or robots to use Ford and Urban's (1963) term.

The goal of instruction is the completion and mastery of predetermined common learnings by all students. Individualized instruction is viewed as an ideal strategy for pupil progress, and students are directed through a common program at their own rate. The use of feedback and other reinforcement devices are emphasized.

Diagnosis and ongoing assessment are recommended to insure proper placement of learners. For those learners who are "behind" or who are not progressing according to expectation, the tutoring relationship is seen as valuable. In addition, small group target teaching and remedial endeavors are employed by the teacher.

In summary, the instructional behavior of the Design A teacher is identifiable according to the following points:

1. Transmission of verifiable facts which constitute universal skills is necessary.

2. Management of children is necessary to ensure proper growth.

3. The teacher should portray a role that reflects a preconceived model of teacher.

4. Children should portray a role that reflects a preconceived model of student.

5. Diagnostic and prescriptive teaching are absolute necessities.

6. Students are allowed to progress through the common curriculum at a rate compatible with their ability range.

7. The common program is divided into carefully sequenced lessons.

8. Ongoing assessment, immediate feedback, and various reinforcement techniques are used to insure that students remain task-oriented.

9. The ends of instructional activities are expressed in highly explicit behavioral terms.

10. Remediation through tutorial and other arrangements is seen as necessary.

11. Instructional attempts are made to accentuate commonalities and minimize differences.

Curriculum. To the Design A teacher, the curriculum is highly structured and content centered; consequently, it is predetermined and logical. For example, fourth grade content must be mastered before a child can be successful with fifth grade content. Activities or lessons are carefully worked out in basic skills and content areas, and sequences of work are carefully planned.

In the final analysis, the curriculum is that part of the school's program that nurtures intellectual discipline. It consists of a common core of subject matter, intellectual skills, and accepted values that are so essential they must be transmitted to all who come to school.

In summary curriculum according to Design A could be exemplified in the following manner:

1. The curriculum is a general education curriculum.

2. The curriculum must place top priority on skills and knowledges necessary for all people to meet the basic demands of society.

3. The school curriculum and the objectives of the school have a direct relationship with the larger society.

4. Day-by-day lesson plan objectives must be well defined and specific.

5. Sequence in curriculum content must indicate that there is a logical structural sequence to knowledge.

6. The curriculum sequence and scope is divided into segmented, isolated, and compartmentalized packages of knowledge specified by grade levels and with predetermined standards applying equally to all children.

7. Elements of the curriculum are derived from the substance of knowledge itself.

8. The curriculum should be considered a totally predetermined body of content with highly defined and restricted delimitations.

Organization. The organizational structure for Design A is founded in three assumptions: (1) schools are designed to inculcate a specific body of subject matter; (2) this subject matter should be identified and rigorously prescribed, and (3) individual differences merely determine one's chances to cover the predetermined content. The pattern of vertical school structure is laid out in grades, each grade specifying the content to be taught. The pattern of horizontal school structure leans toward departmentalization and homogeneous grouping based on subject-matter achievement. Nonpromotion is the primary mechanism by which children who progress slowly are adjusted to the system (NESP, 1961).

The graded form and/or levels approach of school organization was created to serve (1) the educational

24

function of classifying content, and (2) the administrative function of classifying pupils for upward progression through the school. Organization for Design A necessitates determining content for graded tests, questions for graded achievement tests, and grade level expectations. These grade level expectations have become a part of our culture.

In summary, decisions concerning school organization which are congruent with Design A are reflected below:

1. Schools are committed to predetermined standards. The organization of the school reflects a system whereby each child must measure up to a given level of performance. If children do not, they receive a low grade or are retained in a grade or level for an additional period of time until the expected level of performance is achieved.

2. The horizontal organization of the school permits students to be assigned to instructional groups of like ability within subject matter areas. This usually results in a departmentalized arrangement along with an emphasis on homogeneous grouping.

3. Individual differences are usually viewed as existing between and among learners as opposed to differences existing within individual students.

4. Educational prescriptions, the result of elaborate diagnosis, are highly explicit in terms of tasks to be performed within designated study sequences.

5. The teaching function becomes one of diagnosing, prescribing, treating, analyzing results and writing the next prescription. Much attention is paid to learning management systems. There is an emphasis on a high level of accountability for getting desired results.

6. Paraprofessionals are often employed to handle routine tasks.

7. Special teaching personnel are also employed to either assume responsibility for or to assist in diagnosing and providing remedial services.

8. Space arrangement attempts to reflect the instructional plan. Provisions are made to allow smaller spaces for discussion groups. There also is a push for specialized facilities such as laboratories and workshops. Individual study carrels and stations are seen as desirable.

Resources. Each piece of equipment and individual supplies can be justified only to the extent of their overall attainment of previously determined purposes of the school. Resources reflecting Design A are:

1. Materials that correlate with a diagnostic approach and that can be easily prescribed such as programmed materials, teaching machines, subject matter programs, learning packets, and kits are seen as desirable.

2. There is an emphasis on appropriate diagnostic devices.

3. Since the prescribed curriculum is the same for all, there is a tendency toward a single textbook approach, i.e. basal reading series.

General Physical Description. The Design A school is probably somewhat quieter than the so-called more progressive school. The movement of children is scheduled upon the need of the lesson to be covered. Children generally sit at individual desks. Formality is the key to utilization of physical space.

Persons in this environment are expected to assume appropriate roles, (student, teacher, principal, aide) and are expected to exhibit behavior complimentary to the designated role function. The strategy for establishing this type environment results in designing techniques and establishing management goals for the purpose of controlling the individual and maintaining social order. Essentially the plan is for

26

individuals to perform defined functions in predictable situations. Children are expected to respect constituted authority.

In summary:

1. Persons, big and little, are expected to display behavior appropriate to their assigned role.

2. The emphasis is on order, control and management of individuals and of the physical environment; the noise level is kept minimal.

3. A definite plan for learning management is realized through arrangement of the material characteristics of the physical environment.

Evaluation. The process of evaluation is viewed by Design A advocates as a necessary part of the teaching-learning situation. Evaluation is necessary in order that a determination of children's levels of performance are ascertained so that reasonable decisions can be made about their future educational activities. This system is extremely product oriented. The measurement of facts and content is imperative in the evaluation of student learning. The system determines the evaluation methods, and the teacher imposes these procedures upon children.

Evaluation as practiced by proponents of Design A may be summarized as follows:

1. Academic standards serve the purpose of determining preordained adult roles of children, through a policy of inclusion and exclusion in certain aspects of the formal school curriculum.

2. Expecting children to measure up to a given level of performance is the standard form of the evaluation scheme.

3. Predetermined standards apply indiscriminately to all children in a grade or school.

4. National norms are applied to all communities within a state.

27

5. Predetermined standards tend to solidify curriculum structure and learning experiences.

6. Children are placed in learning environments that are best suited for them. This placement is based on someone's assessment of their maturity, abilities, attainment, and over-all general nature.

7. Children are ranked in terms of the success of other children.

8. Knowledge of facts should and must be measured.

Summary

This section presented a brief discussion of both the psychological and philosophical base of Design A. Assumptions concerning beliefs relative to the definition of humans, motivation, learning conditions, social learning, intellectual development, knowledge and society from this particular point of view were listed for contemplation by the reader. A discussion of instructional behavior, curriculum, organizational design, resources, general physical descriptions and evaluation procedures congruent with the beliefs of Design A followed.

Section IV

DESIGN B

Education by Design B is based in Cognitive-field psychology and in Pragmatism and Experimentalism, schools of educational philosophy. Pragmatism as a formal school philosophy is a modern movement which originated in the intellectually and socially turbulent years at the end of the nineteenth and beginning of the twentieth centuries (Marler, 1975).

Cognitive-field theory or psychology is based upon the thinking of Kurt Lewin. The psychology represents a relativistic, as opposed to an absolutistic, mechanistic manner of viewing humans and the learning process. Relativism means that psychological reality is defined in subjective, perceptual terms and not in objective, physical terms. From this definition then, a person's ". . . reality consists of what one makes of that which one gains through one's senses or otherwise" (Bigge, 1964, p. 176).

The heart of Lewin's psychological pursuits centered in the motivating conditions of person-environment situations. He was interested in democratic ideals and practices.

Jerome Bruner (1960) is also considered a Cognitive-field psychologist. He conceptualized the "spiral curriculum" which emphasizes that children can learn at their own level any subject matter at any age and that educators can settle for incomplete, intuitive understanding at intermediate stages of learning. Bruner believes that full knowledge and understanding come with repeated attacks, at increasingly mature levels, on the same topics. The concept of categorizing behavior has been studied by Bruner. Bruner (1957) introduced the term "coding system" to describe the way that the organism learns to code situations which are encountered and how this may lead to appropriate behavior in relation to them. Therefore, all problem-solving behavior implies that the problem has been coded in some way. Bruner proposes that those coding systems should be taught which permit the greatest application to the solving of new problems.

Cognitive development, according to Piaget (1969), is the intellectual concept of biological adaptation

29

to the environment. Wadsworth (1971) explains that as individuals adapt biologically to their environments they also adapt intellectually, organizing and structuring their external world through assimilation and accommodation. Adaptation begins at birth with the exercise of sensory-motor reflexes but as children develop, the adaptations they make are increasingly less related to sensory and motor behaviors alone. Piaget (1969) stressed that knowledge is not transmitted directly but is constructed.

Therefore, teachers, counselors, or school administrators adhering to the tenets of Cognitive-field psychology place great emphasis upon individuals and their interactions with their environment. Providing sequential, growth-producing experiences for all students is of great import in the school based in Design B. Democratic values are stressed in order that students will become productive citizens as adults.

Pragmatism basically represents an American philosophical development although parallel ideas were presented by England's Schiller and Balfour and Germany's Vaihinger. The forerunner of pragmatic thought can be found in Heraclitus, a Greek philosopher who emphasized the constancy of change; in the Sophists, who denied the possibility of knowing ultimate reality; and in Quintilian, the Roman who emphasized action rather than deductive reasoning as a pathway to learning.

In America, the focus of Pragmatism was the harmonizing of the individual and society. The work of William James caught the attention of John Dewey, who is considered the Father of Experimentalism, a branch of Pragmatism. Dewey professed that the process of education provided the proper testing ground for philosophical theory. His works emphasized the individual and stressed activity for activity's sake, rather than for evaluation.

Some of the basic tenets (Dawson, 1976) associated with this particular philosophy of education are:

1. The importance of individual differences and interests of children.

2. Providing alternatives so that the child has the opportunity to experience freedom of choice and concomitant responsibility.

3. The stressing of the scientific method
    of thought and learning.

4. Knowledge is considered to be based in
    experience.

5. Truth is relative; the ultimate questions
    of life cannot be answered as absolutes
    of fixed truths.

6. Children's psychological needs are para-
    mount over the logical order of subject
    matter.

7. Values are instrumental.

Therefore, teachers, counselors, or school administrators adhering to the tenets of Pragmatism/Expe-
rimentalism provide an activity-centered curriculum
in which choice is inherent and problem solving is
prized. Emphasis is placed on children and their
needs. When needs are met, growth continues and
therefore the child progresses toward the realization
of potential. Education must serve as a source of new
ideas for enriching society.

Basic Beliefs: Are Your's Similar?

The Definition of Humans. Advocates of Design B
tend to view humans according to the basic tenets of
Cognitive-field psychology and the philosophical beliefs expressed in Pragmatism/Experimentalism. The
reader is encouraged to take a personal stand on the
following assumptions relative to a definition of
humans:

1. Human behavior is based on cognition,
    the act of knowing or thinking about
    a situation and not on the situation
    itself.

2. Personal cognitive structure is deter-
    mined by experience with the environment
    and the maturation of innate potential.

3. Humans are best described in relative
    terms.

31

4. Human variability is seen as desirable
   in a democratic society which respects
   the dignity and worth of each individual.

5. Humans are endowed with a creative urge
   for improvement.

6. Humans are active, goal-seeking organisms.

7. The human is a social being.

8. Growth and the willingness to change are
   prerequisites to individual freedom.

If you were in agreement with the above assumptions then you probably lean toward a neutral belief of humans. Teachers subscribing to these assumptions begin with children where they are currently functioning, and manipulate the environment so that the best possible experiences occur, based upon teacher's perception of what is best. The total person is one who is in harmony with the external environment.

Motivation. Motivation plays a central role in the learning process. Do you agree or disagree with the following assumptions concerning motivation?

1. Learning experiences are optimal when
   purposes and needs are reasonable,
   meaningful, and appear useful to the
   learner.

2. Productive learning experiences require
   active involvement.

3. Productive learning takes place when
   the tasks are adjusted to the maturity
   and experiential background of the
   learner.

4. Cognitive processes are set into motion
   (thinking) when learners encounter an
   obstacle, difficulty, puzzle or chal-
   lenge in a course of action which interests them.

5. When an individual's psychological and
   emotional needs are met, learning and
   retention will be enhanced.

32

If you were in agreement with the above assumptions, then you probably see the teaching function as a blend of the teacher as a manipulator and the intellectual structures that characterize what is to be taught.

Learning Conditions. What do you believe concerning the conditions best suited for learning? Take a moment to contemplate the following assumptions:

1. Expectations of learners should be based upon knowledge of their abilities which are affected by psychological, social, and emotional development.

2. Learning experiences which have relevance to a child's life will enhance retention, transfer, and usability of knowledge.

3. Experiencing too much disequilibrium causes children's behavior to be less integrated, purposeful and rational.

4. When learners see results, have knowledge of their status and progress and/or achieve insight, understanding and personal meaning, then the learning process proceeds in the best manner.

5. The educative process begins with learners identifying their own concerns and interests.

6. Self concept is related to one's capacity for learning and for making important choices affecting one's learning.

Those who subscribe to these assumptions focus on a combination of self confidence, physiological, social, and intellectual development in determining learner expectations. They are also concerned with whether or not learning tasks are lifelike and/or functional.

Social Learning. Below is a list of assumptions which you may wish to consider as you attempt to delineate beliefs concerning social learning; the acquisition of attitudes and behaviors that enable an individual to function as a member of society.

1. Children learn much from one another.

2. Children receive satisfaction from work, gain a sense of worthiness, experience stimulation, and enjoy the process, when confronted with reasonable challenges.

3. Satisfaction in learning is affected by the group atmosphere as well as the product.

4. Every human cultural system is logical and coherent in its own terms.

5. Humans have the capacity to adopt, adapt and reconstitute present and past ideas and beliefs. Humans also have the capabilities to create.

Those who subscribe to these assumptions emphasize how the individual functions relative to group norms. They see satisfaction in learning affected by the group atmosphere as well as by products.

Intellectual Development. What do you believe concerning the development of the intellect? Take a few moments to reflect on the following assumptions:

1. Intelligence test scores of individual children can be positively affected by felt need to achieve, personal initiative, and aggressiveness.

2. Tests cannot adequately measure innate capacity.

3. The most rapid mental growth occurs during infancy and early childhood; children achieve approximately half of their total mental growth by the age of five.

4. Ability to learn increases with age up to adult years.

5. Learning readiness is a result of the "proper mix" of emotional, social, physiological, and intellectual growth of the child.

6. Differences in intelligence are more influenced by learned cultural patterns than genetically inherited characteristics.

7. Children learn and develop intellectually not only at their own rate but in their own style.

If you tend to agree with these assumptions then you probably agree with those who submit that readiness for learning is a complex interplay of social, physiological, emotional, and intellectual development. The focus is on learning style as well as learning rate.

Knowledge. How would you define knowledge? Are knowing and knowledge one and the same? Take a few moments to ponder the assumptions listed below:

1. Knowledge is temporary and conditional.

2. Knowledge is rooted in experience. Experience may be either immediate or meditated.

3. Humans create knowledge as they interact with the total environment.

4. Information becomes knowledge when it is thought to be relevant to the solution of a particular problem.

5. Workability is the test of truth.

Those adhering to these assumptions assert that knowledge is rooted in experience, and therefore is tentative. As children grow, develop, and change, knowledge of what is true also changes. Information becomes knowledge when it is considered relevant to the solution of a particular problem.

Society. The final set of assumptions for this section are relative to the concept of society. How would you define society? What influence does society have on the growth and development of individuals?

1. Society is a process in which individuals participate.

2. Education is a social program that is constantly undergoing reconstruction.

3. The school is one of society's resources for social experimentation.

4. Society is self renewing.

5. Society gives order and direction to human behavior.

Those agreeing with these assumptions see society as a process in which individuals participate. The major role of the school is to teach the adults of the future to deal with the planning necessary in the process called society. Education must serve as a source of new ideas.

Again, to suggest that one individual's beliefs relative to a philosophy of education exist in an either/or situation or pure form is not our intent. However, we again emphasize that educators possess beliefs that cause them to lean toward certain philosophic postures. If your reactions to the sets of assumptions did not reveal a tendency toward an identifiable profile, we strongly suggest further study on your part.

In any event, in order for philosophical/theoretical propositions to provide a degree of utility they ultimately must be translated into educational practices. The following segment of this section reflects this effort. Educational practices reflecting Design B have been established for the following variables (1) Instruction, (2) Curriculum, (3) Organization, (4) Content, (5) Materials and Resources, (6) Classification of Learners, (7) General Physical Description, and (8) Evaluation.

Educational Practices

Instruction. "Not the age but the stage" is a cliche that has come to be associated with Design B. As Goodlad (1965) points out:

Children are different, much more different than we have up to now recognized. . . . The usual fourth-grade class contains children achieving at second, third, fourth,

fifth and sixth grades in some aspects of
their schoolwork--and even occasionally
above and below these levels (p. 57).

Teachers in Design B are primarily concerned with
determining the current educational status of individuals and providing the necessary courses to be followed for them to successfully progress through the
curriculum. Diagnosis and prescription on an individual basis is seen as ideal. The role of the teacher
becomes one of a learning manager and consultant whose
primary task is to orchestrate the learning environment.

Although curriculum units are not necessarily
prescribed, the teacher has a plan or an idea for the
week or day, with specific areas that are to be
covered. In addition, there is a general plan to be
completed in the classroom during the day. This planning is in terms of individuals as well as the class
as a whole. If children lose interest, the teacher
redirects their attention in attempting to arouse
their curiosity in a parallel activity. The teacher
keeps individual progress records on children, so
that proper placement in relation to their rates of
development can be made in each curricular area.

Purdom (1970) points out that the teacher model
according to Design B is not necessarily restricted to
human instruction. Currently, programmed texts and
teaching machines have assumed some of the teacher
functions. Teacher performance is a result of applying appropriate techniques.

Instruction as practiced by teachers advocating
Design B may be summarized as follows:

1. The teacher functions as a resource
    person to individuals and groups rather
    than as a taskmaster.

2. Subgrouping for instructional purposes
    is recommended.

3. Learning activities are appropriately
    phased. The teacher decides when it is
    time to summarize or to pull loose ends
    together before moving on to another
    aspect of that which is to be learned.

4. The study period is well-organized with children knowing what is expected of them.

5. Educational listening, viewing, and reading opportunities present themselves in a vast array of television programs, films, filmstrips, pictures, books, and magazines.

6. Learning activities are provided on the basis of individual needs.

7. Children are assisted in progressing through the curriculum sequence at their own rate of development.

   Curriculum. Design B proponents support the idea that learning experiences should be developed differently for each child. Academic skills in reading, writing, and math use an integrated curriculum design. Learning to read usually follows a language experience approach. However, some teachers introduce phonics to help break down new words or basal readers to reinforce skill development. Mathematics is taught by using concrete objects--things to count, weigh, measure, and through activities related to everyday living.

   Time is spent teaching skills even though focus lies primarily with conceptual learning. When experiences are created for the student by the teacher, the need for learning skills becomes apparent to the child.

   The curriculum is designed around the key concepts, values, and skills of the various disciplines. Broad structural aspects provide continuity of learning.

   The curriculum in a Design B school focuses on four attributes: (1) balance, (2) content selection, (3) spiral, and (4) structure. Balance in curriculum is maintained for the learner through attempting to diminish those deficiencies being experienced by the child. To determine balance in the curriculum, it becomes necessary to distinguish between content and subject matter that can be designated as cultural imperatives and cultural electives.

The spiral curriculum is supported by the premise that children need to reinforce and supplement their behaviors before moving on to the next level of learning. This approach affords the learner time to associate meaning with newly acquired information.

In order to predict, direct, diagnose, and assess the cognitive growth of individual children, logical sequence of content must be applied to the curriculum. This facilitates the function of student placement in the curriculum experience.

Curriculum by Design B may be summarized as follows:

1. Top priority is placed on skills and knowledge necessary for all people to meet the basic demands of life.

2. Content earns its place in the curriculum by its contribution to the achievement of educational objectives.

3. The spiral curriculum is viewed as a useful procedure for providing time for the learner to conceptualize by moving from narrow perceptivity to global perceptivity.

4. The horizontal aspect (scope) of the curriculum provides for a variety of unifying learning experiences.

5. The curriculum organization utilizes systematic structure with both pre-determined and emergent learning activities.

6. Provisions are made for the interdisciplinary nature of knowledge.

7. Balance in the curriculum is determined by analyzing both societal and personal needs and expressing these as curriculum needs.

8. An emphasis on a national curriculum encourages a system of articulation among schools, within school systems, and among states.

Organization. Design B advocates place as priority an organizational scheme which provides for differential rates and means of progression or growth.
The vertical organization of the school should provide
for continuous, fluid upward progression of all learners. The horizontal organization permits flexibility
in placing pupils in instructional groups that vary in
size from one to multiple numbers. Since it is accepted that children grow, develop, and learn at different rates, the notions of retention, retardation, or
failure are virtually nonexistent.

Differential staffing or at least some form of
team teaching is seen as desirable in Design B. It is
more convenient to offer instructional assistance to
students because arrangements can be made to free
individuals in the team to work with groups ranging
from one child to multiple numbers.

Therefore, the organization of the school based
in Design B is summarized as follows:

1. Human varability among learners is
   accommodated through vertical organization which provides for continuous
   upward progression of all learners.

2. When assigning children to learning
   groups, the instructional style of
   the teacher, learning style of the
   child, and learning goals to be
   achieved are all considered.

3. The horizontal organization of the
   school provides flexibility for
   individual, small, and large group
   arrangements.

4. Groups of teachers responsible for
   clusters of children meet and plan
   in an attempt to articulate learning
   activities.

5. Group or team planning by teachers
   encourages the identification and
   utilization of special talents pos-
   sessed by individual teachers.

6. The contributions of specilized personnel are seen as an integral part
   of the total educational program as
   opposed to something separate.

7. An argument given for team teaching
   is that a group of teachers are more
   apt to represent a balance of effective skills or competencies than a
   single teacher in a self contained
   unit. (Sloan, 1964).

Content. Content priorities have been established for education in America for as long as schools
have existed. At the present time schools are criti-
cized if children do not have a supply of traditional
knowledge, are poor or inadequate citizens, lack
family living skills, lack skills or knowledge to become employed, or if their values are different from
the previous generation.

The school has assumed these burdens and has
attempted in varying degrees to meet these challenges.
What tasks have the Design B advocates identified?
These can be summarized as follows: (1) acquisition
of certain cognitive skills through subjects such as
English, mathematics, and science; (2) acquisition
of social skills and appropriate behavioral patterns;
(3) acquisitions of personal human relations skills
in order to deal with basic human interactions; (4)
acquisition of necessary vocational skills; and (5)
acquisition of a value system which is acceptable to
the larger society. In summary:

1. Content contributes to the achievement
   of educational objectives or the mission
   of the school.

2. Sequence in content reflects a logical
   structural sequence to knowledge and
   to development.

3. There should be a balance between the
   content-centered curriculum and the
   process curriculum.

Materials and Resources. Since Design B is
anchored in human variability theory, advocates emphasize the provision of a wide range of materials and
resources. There are few textbooks, as such, in sets:

41

instead, there are trade and reference works and audio visual aids. People in the community are seen as potential resources.

Very often centralized resource centers are established based on the rationale that such an area reduces the need for duplication of resources, that a wider range of materials is available and that greater access to these materials is possible.

Classification of Learners or Grouping. Teachers in Design B schools are primarily concerned with determining the current academic status of children and mapping out necessary educational experiences to insure that they experience successful progress. Achievement grouping is the most popular means through which this is accomplished.

The content is usually sequenced into a series of instructional levels, each level building on the other. Children are then assigned to instructional groups which best meet the needs of their particular achievement levels in the content areas. This type of grouping is especially prevalent in the areas of math and reading. Such pupil classification provides children with the opportunity of progressing through the sequenced content at their own rates. Organizational schemes that use this method of classifying pupils are nongraded, individually prescribed instruction and individually guided education.

Children are grouped and regrouped on the basis of objectives, achievement and whatever criteria best fit a particular learning situation. For example, overlapping the reading level from group to group permits greater flexibility. If children are rapid learners, they can periodically move into new groups which are more advanced. If children learn slowly, they may stay with the same group for an extended period of time, thus receiving the attention they need.

In summary:

1. Attempts are made to assign children to instructional groups that are compatible with their needs, interests, and achievement levels.

42

2. Prestructured materials and learning activities that reflect clearly defined learning objectives are provided in order to facilitate the learner's individual rate of progress.

3. Intra-individual differences within children are provided for through flexible grouping arrangements.

4. Grade labels are removed or minimized.

5. Chidren progress according to their own developmental pattern.

6. There is no need for retention, retardation, or failure.

7. Goals are set individually so that children may learn as rapidly as they are able, within the pattern which best suits their own particular rate of development.

8. Interest grouping is an important dimension of the organizational pattern. Children are encouraged to pursue special interest activities on either an individual or group basis; provisions are made either within the regular classroom or special resource center.

9. Self-instructional work areas are provided.

10. Each cluster of children includes multiple age groups.

11. It is important for at least one adult in the school to know and understand each child well.

Time and Space. Design B teachers see value in a basic time schedule since effective learning cannot take place in a school that is random in nature. For learning to proceed with order and harmony, some scheduling of activities is necessary.

The use of bells is minimized. There are however, fixed time divisions to insure order. The
traffic of individual children shifting and regrouping
is not seen as a problem. Therefore, time and space
utilization in Design B is a function of planned
learning activities resulting in flexible time sched-
ules.

General Physical Description. Generally, there
are no individual desks and children do not have assigned places. Rooms are equipped with tables for
ease in providing various kinds of activities.
Alcoves often are created with book cases and other
moveable furniture. These secluded areas often are
called corners, learning centers or learning stations.
There is usually a math center, a reading center, an
art center, as well as centers for other activities.
If the teacher has a desk it is generally placed in
an out of the way part of the room.

The teacher usually works with one group of children at at time while other groups are occupied in
independent work. There is little teaching, as such,
to the whole group.

In summary, the general physical description of
the school based on Design B may be summarized as
follows:

1. The overall environment reflects a
   busy and industrious atmosphere with
   students working at relevant tasks
   that provide them with success.

2. The teacher guides by moving from
   group to group to either serve as
   resource person or to keep children
   task oriented.

Evaluation. Design B reflects a belief that any
evaluation system in which pupils are ranked in terms
of the success of other children will create more un-
wholesome competition than will a system in which success of others is not necessarily related to one's
own. Advocates of Design B emphasize that the uniform
standards approach fails to consider human variability.

Design B evaluation programs have three dimen-
sions: (1) quantitative measurements, (2) the
teacher's judgment, and (3) the child's feelings. The

third dimension considers children's attitudes and feelings toward themselves and their academic work. Proponents of Design B believe that the best approach to assessing growth is to consider the child's actual performance. In reporting and evaluating, the teacher describes what the child is doing. Such basic, analytical description is more meaningful than any grade symbol. Since the school's goal is to develop the total child, evaluation reflects that effort. The ability of the child to comprehend and recall facts is valuable, but only as it provides a point of reference from which higher levels of cognition may proceed.

Evaluation, according to Design B, must be quantitative, qualitative, and predictive to be of real value. Such criteria can be met only through subjective and objective evaluation by the teacher plus the child's own reflective evaluation. Evaluation must determine: (1) if enough preliminary knowledge is available for the child to proceed; (2) if the child is able to grow effectively and to produce in the environment; (3) if the child has the opportunity for higher order learning; and (4) the most important, if the child's concept of self gives any indication that the first three criteria are being met.

Therefore, evaluation based in Design B emphasizes that the best theoretical approach to assessing growth is to consider the child's actual performance. This basic and analytical description is more meaningful than any grade, regardless of the symbols used.

Summary

This section presented the basic beliefs and the concomitant educational practices inherent in Design B; an approach to education founded in Cognitive-field psychology and in the philosophy of Pragmatism/Experimentalism. Readers were asked to compare their beliefs and practices with those of Design B advocates.

45

Section V

DESIGN C

Education by Design C has its roots in Humanistic psychology and Existential philosophy. Humanistic psychology focuses on "man himself--his needs, his goals, his achievements, his success. . ." (Goble, 1970, p. xii). The human potential movement is often referred to as the Third Force and has become a voice in education that is beginning to be heard over the cries of the technologist, portrayed in Design A, and those of the Experimentalist, depicted in Design B.

Abraham Maslow, Rollo May, Fredrick Perls and Carl Rogers are among the most notable psychologists associated with Humanistic psychology. According to these persons, the single basic motivation of all human beings is the actualization of one's potentials (Patterson, 1973). An individual's specific needs are organized (Maslow, 1959) and assume temporary priority relative to this basic need for self-actualization. A specific need which is temporarily most important receives attention or becomes the figure against the ground of other needs, to use Gestalt terminology.

Therefore, the concept of threat becomes very important in the learning process. Humanistic psychologists believe that threat leads to resistance to change; that threat will not lead to self-enhancing behavior, but to self-preserving behavior. According to Combs and Snygg (1959) learning or positive behavior does not occur under threat, and therefore it becomes increasingly important to consider those conditions which minimize threat and which lead to positive behavior change.

Rogers (1957, 1961) has delineated conditions or aspects of personal relationships which minimize threat or the need to protect oneself and which therefore, maximize self-enhancing behaviors. Three of the basic conditions are: (1) empathic understanding, (2) respect or nonpossessive warmth and (3) genuineness. A brief description may clarify the meaning of these conditions. Empathy, according to Rogers (1961, p. 284), is ". . . to sense the (other's private world as if it were your own, but without losing the 'as if' quality . . .)" The Cherokee Indians generally are

47

credited with a prayer that expresses the concept of empathy. The last phrase is: ". . . have walked the trail of life in his moccasins." Empathy, therefore, is the ability and the sensitiveness to perceive and feel from another's point of view.

Nonpossessive warmth or respect is a second condition necessary for minimizing threat and maximizing self-enhancing behaviors. Inherent in this concept is an acceptance of the other as a person of worth without judgment or condemnation.

Genuineness connotes openness, honesty and sincerity. Rogers (1957) states that a genuine person is freely and deeply himself and therefore, he is without a facade. Many Existential philosophers refer to the genuine person as one who is authentic.

Rogers (1977) discusses the fundamental conditions that may be observed when person-centered learning develops in a school. He states:

> The political implications of person-centered education are clear: the student retains his power and control over himself; he shares in the responsible choices and decisions; the facilitator provides the climate for these aims (p. 74).

Humanistic psychologists, therefore, focus on the loving, positive, creative and healthy individual. May (1969, p. 289) eloquently states: "Care is a state in which something does matter; care is the opposite of apathy. Care is . . . the source of human tenderness. Fortunate, indeed, is it that care is born in the same act as the infant." The potential of man is unlimited from the humanistic perspective.

Existentialism is a modern twentieth century philosophy which is often credited to Kierkegaard, a philosopher-psychologist-theologian. Much confusion exists in attempting to state an Existential philosophy for most Existentialists do not choose to be labeled as such. Marler (1975) states that Existentialism as a philosophic system has been an influence in public education since the 1940's. This influence has been a protest focusing on a depersonalization of man in mass society. The Humanistic psychologists, Maslow, Fromm, May, Kelley, Combs and Rogers, have attempted to translate Existential thought into education and counseling realities.

According to Morris (1961), the Existentialists believe that the ultimate questions of life cannot be answered with finality, however, trying to answer them is what life is all about. The Existentialist aim of education is to understand oneself first of all (Green, 1967). Basic tenets of Existentialism presented by Bates and Johnson (1972) may help the reader clarify Existential thought as applied to the educational process.

1. Existence precedes essence.

   Humans exist and must define themselves. Living is a process of self definition.

2. Humans are condemned to freedom.

   Only when humans use the sentence of freedom to make conscious choices are they alive. Humans must choose for themselves and accept full responsibility for the consequences of those choices. Being aware of implications of freedom, Existential humans stand up to it as best they can.

3. When humans choose, they choose for all humans.

   As humans make choices they are aware that they are the only representative of humankind they will ever truly know and therefore, inherent in choices are implications that these choices are best for all humans.

4. Humans define themselves through their actions.

   Humans define themselves only through what they do not by what they say they are going to do nor what they intend to do. According to Existentialists the final relevancy is action. Feelings are relevant and worth exploration only in understanding the barriers to action.

5. Two worlds exist -- the world of objective reality and the world of subjective
   reality.

       A world of objective reality exists
   and is more or less knowable by scientific laws to humans. However, a world
   of subjective reality governed by more
   or less unknown psychological laws
   exists and is only tentatively knowable
   by humans.

A brief discussion of Humanistic psychology and
Existential philosophy have been presented as the
roots of education for Design C.

Basic Beliefs: Are Your's Similar?

The Definition of Humans. Readers are encouraged
to contemplate either agreement or disagreement with
the following basic assumptions relative to their
definition of humans:

1. Humans are described meaningfully
   in terms of their consciousness.

2. Humans are greater than the sum of
   their parts.

3. Humans define their potential through
   choices.

4. Individual perceptions are the only
   reality known to humans.

5. Humans are free when they choose
   responsibly.

6. Basic human values are a direct
   examination of a person's nature
   and are not relative.

7. Humans can only be studied as a
   whole.

8. Humans have an inherent tendency
   toward self-actualization and pro-
   ductivity.

If you were in agreement with these assumptions then you are probably in accord with those who believe humans are inherently inclined toward goodness. Humans are seen as cooperative and constantly seeking experiences that enhance their unique selves. Individual perceptions are the only reality known to humans.

Motivation. All educators function with some basic beliefs concerning motivation. Since motivation plays a central role in the learning process, it is imperative that educators clarify their beliefs in this important area:

1. The desire to learn comes from within the individual.

2. True learning occurs when the experience is internalized and becomes a part of the child's total being.

3. The level of aspiration set by the learner affects the learning process and achievement.

4. Children possess natural curiosity and will more effectively explore and internalize their environment without adult interference.

5. Exploratory behavior is self-perpetuating.

6. Children who understand and who are involved in what they are doing can create their own methods of accomplishing educational tasks.

Individuals agreeing with these assumptions regard persons as initiators of their own learning tasks. The most desirable rewards are internal in nature and are a reflection of self satisfaction.

Learning Conditions. What do you consider the essential requirements necessary for learning to take place? How do people learn? Respond to the assumptions listed below and test your beliefs relative to conditions of learning against those inherent in Design C:

51

1. Children display natural exploratory behavior when threat is absent.

2. Learning emerges in the flow and continuity of human experiencing and growing (MacDonald, Wolfson, and Zaret, 1973, p. 8).

3. Play and work are synonomous activities for young children.

4. Children are perceptually closer to learning situations that meet their needs than are teachers; subsequently, they have an intuitive feeling for what is needed and are capable of self direction.

5. When children understand the purpose of the activity in which they are engaged, their cognitive curiosity becomes extensive.

Those who subscribe to these assumptions recognize that the learner is perceptually closer to the learning situation than are teachers: subsequently, they see and feel what is needed and are capable of self-direction. Learning emerges in the flow and continuity of man's total experiencing and growing. There cannot be stated outcomes of learning (MacDonald, Wolfram, and Zaret, 1973).

Social Learning. How do children acquire the attitudes and behaviors that allow them to function as members of society? Below is a list of assumptions which the reader may wish to consider:

1. Humans are social beings who seek active involvement with others.

2. Humans create their own environment.

3. Humans tend to select groups which agree with their own beliefs; there is a tendency to break off contact with contradictory views.

If you agree with these assumptions then you probably accept that humans create their own environment. Individuals are central to their own idiosyncratic universe.

Intellectual Development. Take a few moments to consider the following assumptions relative to intellectual development as advocated by Design C proponents:

1. The less planned adult intervention, the greater intellectual gains of the child.

2. The majority of children possess far more native intelligence than can be ascertained by current behavioral measures; consequently, the concern is with releasing potential capacity as opposed to being preoccupied with that which can be identified.

3. Verbal abstractions should follow direct experience with objects and ideas, not precede nor substitute for them.

According to persons subscribing to Design C, intellectual development proceeds from "wholes" to "parts" or from a simplified whole to more complex wholes. Intellectual potential already exists within the individual as opposed to a phenomenon to be developed or realized.

Knowledge. Is knowledge understanding, acquaintance with facts or awareness? Once again the reader is asked to react to a set of assumptions:

1. Knowledge is a model created by the individual that makes sense out of encounters with the external conditions in the environment.

2. The process associated with the development of new knowledge and new insights is greater in significance than simply the act of receiving or transmitting knowledge.

3. Knowledge is personal.

4. A universal body of knowledge necessary for all to know does not exist.

5. How children feel about what they know is equally as important as what they know.

Design C advocates submit that the only certainty of humans is that they experience streams of thoughts and feelings. Information becomes knowledge only when it takes on personal meaning for the individual. Truth is an individual matter.

Society. The final set of assumptions in this section deals with the concept of society and are presented below:

1. Society has existence in humans' minds.

2. Society provides a system of universals.

3. The school's primary task is individual; an incidental task of the school is social.

Those who subscribe to these assumptions specify that the way to improve society is through improving the quality of individuals, not through improving institutions. The tendency is toward an egalitarian society.

Hopefully, the reader has contemplated the assumptions inherent in Design C relative to the definition of humans, motivation, conditions of learning, social learning, intellectual development, knowledge and society. Readers have now had an opportunity to clarify their beliefs according to the three psychological/philosophical camps presented in the monograph. Are your beliefs more like one of the camps than the others?

The translation of these beliefs into daily educational practice has been left to individual educators and the results often have been disappointing and confusing. The remainder of this section will focus on the translation of Humanistic psychology and Existential philosophy into educational practice.

Educational Practices

Instruction. Advocates of Design C submit that the task in a school environment (learning) is the same for both teacher and student. MacDonald (1968, p. 38) establishes that, "A person is not a bundle of needs or interests, or unique purposes that can be directed or guided or developed to someone's satisfaction." Learning is the lifelong process of acquiring personal meaning. Any educational experience that does not focus on the person must necessarily by relegated to the realm of training and can hardly be classified as an educational experience. According to Design C proponents, the purposes of schooling is to foster the unlimited potential of the child to love, to learn, to create, and to grow.

In order to release children to become whomever they may be, requires a basic trust on the part of teachers of the self-fulfilling potential of human beings. It requires living with the realization that children must handle their own world in their own time; this educators cannot do for children regardless of the noble intentions they might have. Children must be guaranteed the privacy of sorting out what is meaningful to them from their environment. Too often the school represents an overstimulating environment, full of well-meaning, overanxious teachers who seem to be afraid of leaving children alone with their thoughts and perceptions of self in a rapidly changing world. Children need time to assimilate input into some kind of a context that has meaning, purpose, and significance for their lives.

The instructional behavior of the teacher who adheres to Design C is determined by the learner and occurs only by invitation from the learner. Choice is inherent in a Design C teacher's classroom.

In summary, instructional behavior translated from Design C focuses on the following considerations:

1. Children are naturally goal setting persons and enjoy striving toward self-determined goals.

2. Children receive many satisfactions from work, have pride in achievement, enjoy the process, and gain a sense of worthiness from contribution, pleasure in association when they have been actively involved in setting the goals.

3. Children aspire to independence, self-expression, and are capable of learning responsibility for their behavior.

4. Children who are involved to the extent of understanding the purpose of what they are doing can create their own methods of accomplishing educational tasks.

5. Children seek to give meaning to their lives by identifying with certain basic groups.

6. Children naturally dislike routine tasks that are boring and desire new experiences.

7. Children desire to be released, encouraged and assisted.

Learners' needs and interests have priority as the sources for curricular development and learners have the explicit right to develop their uniqueness and individuality. Learners are active in planning their programs. This planning involves the means for pursuing objectives and methods of evaluating choices, as well as the task of identifying objectives. Involvement of this type encourages the practice of behaviors necessary for being an autonomous, self-actualized person.

Curriculum. Curriculum by Design C is dependent upon the potential unfolding and surfacing of an unlimited source of curriculum that lies dormant within the learner's creative reservoir. Academic skills in reading, writing and math are not taught in isolation, but are part of the atmosphere of the room. There is no abdication of the responsibility for giving children the skills that they need, for those skills are seen as tools. Samples and Wohlford (1973) would probably refer to this as "celebrating" the curriculum and Leonard (1968) would probably classify this as the "ecstacy" of learning.

In the final analysis Design C advocates believe one of the most important factors influencing children's successes in school is the amount of influence they have over their environment. This includes choosing when and what and how they are going to study.

Curriculum from the Design C perspective can be summarized as follows:

56

1. A curriculum reflecting an open system
   is considered dynamic and forever
   emerging. This requires a balance
   between input and output.

2. The curriculum should reflect as its
   source, the children of that school.

3. The curriculum environment provides
   each student with multiple options to
   explore; i.e., touch, dream, read,
   count, taste, think, sense, feel,
   tell, and smell.

4. Curriculum structure exists largely
   in teachers' and students' minds,
   not on paper.

Organization. Organization in a Design C school
is predicated on function controlling structure, as
opposed to structure dictating function. Essentially,
this means taking into account the nature of children
and developing an instructional program which allows
rather than restricts growth and development. Emphasis is on the individual.

The right of children to be selective in respect
to that which they attend is a right that must be
respected and cherished in the school. However, in
addition to exercising the right to be selective,
children have the right of access to the Universe
through skills, knowledges, and understanding nurtured
in schools. In schools children have access rights to
all the skills, knowledges and understandings that
provide them with the tools for becoming more aware of
their total Universe.

Organization is adaptive to the circumstances
that occur as a consequence of a time-space blend.
Individual children plan their own use of time within
limits of personal and social order.

In summary, the organization of the Design C
school reflects the following:

1. The organizational design of the school
   is an expression of the needs, wants,
   and desires of its clientele.

2. The organization provides for the interdisciplinary nature of education: no area of knowledge can exist independent of all other areas of knowledge.

3. The organizational scheme of the school should provide opportunity for children to: (1) have access to appropriate information unique to their individual cognitive and affective growth, and (2) have a warm, personal relationship with competent teachers.

4. If specialized personnel are used, their work is coordinated with and related to the total program.

5. In order for each child to experience a sense of belonging there should be a group of children with whom a particular child is somewhat intimate.

6. Individuals and groups should not be restricted by delimited content or courses of study.

7. The organizational structure should not result in "labeling" children at an early age.

8. Children are not grouped according to ability.

9. Each major cluster of children includes multiple ages.

Content. Persons associated with Design C raise several significant questions relative to the content taught in school. Are current curricular programs in schools committed to assisting children in developing and/or acquiring those skills necessary for living a rewarding and fruitful life? What are these life skills? Can they be taught? Are we entering an era where education for work, a vocational emphasis, will be relatively unimportant, and education for life will be crucial? Can life skills be separated into those classified as primary and those that are secondary? Do we educate for actuality or potentiality?

58

Questions of this nature are not new nor unique; however, there is concern as to whether or not they receive serious consideration by those responsible for the education of the young. It is imperative that educators reevaluate the present thrust to ascertain if they are indeed equipping the young with necessary skills for living in an ever transforming world.

Design C educators create educational programs that are concerned with process skills that enable the person to know, to think, to value, to feel, and to act. Berman (1967) defines process skills as those which have an element of ongoingness about them. For too long the educational experiences for children has been approached as if, indeed, it were terminal instead of continuous; i.e., third grade placement, fourth grade content, fifth grade experiences and so on. Therefore, the need to reexamine exactly what constitutes the essentials or basic skills is long overdue, according to Design C proponents.

As a minimum, Design C educators believe that the following process skills are needed in order that each student become a contributing and participating member of society: (1) decision making, (2) communication, (3) interdependent growth, and (4) purposeful structuring of one's own life. Each child needs to know how to make decisions. Educators' approach to decision making according to Design C has been to teach problem solving: however, being sophisticated in problem solving procedures alone does not necessarily guarantee that children will make appropriate decisions. Children need to know to what extent emotions, values, information and risk enter into decisions. Generally, the important decisions people make in life are as much determined by their feelings as by what they know.

In order to live a quality life, it is necessary that children communicate. Typically the school attempts to achieve this goal by teaching language arts. Design C advocates believe that educators must extend their concept of communication to include perception and sensitiveness.

Children also need opportunities for independent growth: This encompasses human relationships in the school. Children should experience giving and receiving. At least one promising approach to achieving this goal is to allow children to work together on tasks.

A most necessary ingredient for quality life is learning how to order and structure one's own life in a purposeful manner. This is a difficult task confronting all people. Children can only learn internal structure in an atmosphere of freedom (Berne, 1964).

If what is important in the Design C school is a quality of life for each child, then the eight priorities identified by Berman (1967) could determine the content of a process-oriented curriculum. The eight process-oriented areas she proposes are:

1. perceiving

2. communicating

3. loving

4. knowing

5. decision making

6. patterning

7. creating

8. valuing

Thus, at the risk of oversimplifying a complex task, we have established the assumption that those process skills identified by Berman serve as a sound base for designing the content of a process-oriented curriculum in the Design C school. We also hypothesize that a youngster who acquires these skills will be equipped to profit from instead of cope with a complex society, or for that matter any society.

The content of the curriculum based in Design C could be summarized as follows:

1. Children do not necesarily behave according to what they know. Only when information takes on personal meaning is the learner affected either positively or negatively.

2. The separate discipline approach to presenting information to children is antithetical to their conception of reality. Before information

becomes knowledge for the child it must undergo personal processing.

3. Knowledge is an idiosyncratic scheme of information and experiences that gives meaning and structure to a child's existence.

4. Little or no knowledge exists which is essential for every child to acquire.

5. Children know more than they can demonstrate behaviorally.

Materials and Resources. In Design C schools there is much use of concrete materials; materials may be inexpensive such as wood scraps, cardboard, boxes, spools, buttons, and so on. However, traditional sources such as textbooks, films and media are also available. Multiple copies of traditional materials as opposed to single sets are available. There are trade books and references works readily available.

In summary, then, the materials and resources of the school founded in Design C are:

1. Resources are limited only by teachers' and children's imaginations.

2. Wide use is made of raw materials, trade books, and reference works.

Classification of Learners. In Design C schools the classification of learners is of low priority. The focus is on humane interactions that reflect mutual interest, compassion, and consideration of others. Design C schools have a major responsibility to nurture humane relations among its constituents, and to give this nurturing intellectual significance. Therefore, in the Design C school an atmosphere is provided that encourages children and teachers to reach inward for their unlimited potential to love, to create, to learn, and to grow.

Classification might be described as the pheno- menon of personal order applied to the process of be- coming and/or growing. We are not speaking of order in the traditional context of rigid structure, but rather of personal order in the sense that a person's position in time and space reflects harmony. In other words, pupils' state of being has purpose, makes sense to them and they have a firm grasp on some sense of self-direction.

Often learners will seek assistance from teachers and peers in formulating learning goals. However, the learner at all times remains an active participant in the planning. Thus classification is a self-selection process initiated by learners as they seek opportunities and activities to fulfill their self-established goals. Therefore, classification of learners is the result of self-selection on the child's part in an environment that encourages the expression of needs in choices.

Time and Space. The utilization of time and space is an expression of personal work habits of individual students. However, for learning to proceed with order and harmony in a Design C school, joint scheduling of some activities is necessary. Except for those activities which involve much noise or movement, there is little need for scheduling to avoid distraction. No time constraints are set for delving into subject matter areas.

In summary:

1. Children plan their own use of time within some parameters.

2. Minimal time constraints are established.

General Physical Description. A key term used in describing the physical environment is "personally involved." At times a child is engaged in deep concentration and at other times is committed to less involved work or relaxation.

Routine is left to the discretion of the teacher and children. Children are given or establish their own options for activities. Furniture ranges from traditional tables, chairs and book cases to stuffy old divans and bean bag chairs. Room arrangements provide for privacy in quiet corners and for space that allows interaction between larger groups. Informality is the key to furniture arrangement.

When children report to school they usually check in with a teacher and then go to work in various locations. For example, one child may want to finish reading a book, six children may be working on a social studies report, five children may be working or dramatizing a story, three children may seek assistance from a peer tutor in developing math skills, and eight children will be working with the teacher on reading skills, and so on. Children are engaged in activities appropriate in accommodating their needs and wants.

The general physical description of a Design C school can be summarized as follows:

1. Rooms are arranged to provide for privacy as well for small and large group interactions.

2. Furniture is arranged informally.

3. The physical environment accomodates multiple learning styles.

Evaluation. Evaluation is solicited by the learner and the norm is self-established. Evaluation data is available to children upon their requests and is a shared experience as opposed to being imposed from without. Children are furnished with data and encouraged to analyze and interpret for themselves.

Since the Design C teacher is process oriented, critical thinking is prized. Evaluation is seen as a cooperative venture and is engaged in when the student asks for feedback.

Evaluation in a Design C school can be summarized as follows:

1. The right-wrong answer syndrome that has permeated much of American education discourages children from risking making mistakes. Making mistakes are essential aspects of learning.

2. Those aspects of a child's learning that do not lend themselves to quantative measurement are too often neglected by teachers.

3. The pressure of objective measures of performance often have detrimental effects upon learning.

4. A teacher's intuitive perceptions of children's behavior is a legitimate body of data to use in assessment.

Summary

This section presented a brief discussion of both the psychological and philosophical bases of education by Design C. Various assumptions concerning beliefs relative to the definition of humans, motivation, learning conditions, social learning, intellectual development, knowledge and society from this particular point of view were presented for contemplation by the reader. A discussion of instructional behavior, curriculum, organizational design, content, materials and resources, classification of learners, time and space, general physical description and evaluation procedures congruent with the beliefs of Humanistic philosophy followed.

Section VI

EPILOGUE:

LANGUAGE AS A DIVERSION TOOL

How does one write a manuscript of this nature without reflecting personal biases? Although we have attempted to demonstrate an objective posture, our beliefs and values have seemed to become evident. We say this not in an apologetic manner but rather from a standpoint of professional integrity.

This has occurred partly because we have used the only tool that we know available for exchanging information about schooling: Language. The reason that we chose philosophic inquiry as the research tool for descriptive analysis is that values and beliefs do not seem to lend themselves entirely to scientific inquiry as a mode of investigation. And whether we like it or not, decisions determining the direction of schooling seem to reflect the belief systems of those who have the power to make such decisions. We hope the manuscript has served as a catalyst to those in power in assisting to clarify their beliefs and ultimately to assist in determining if that which they advocate is really what they desire.

It is as if the "enthusiasm" for power, control, change and innovation, the watchwords of the 60's, were replaced by the "fear" of the 70's and "caution" of the 80's. These movements were and are grounded in emotion and tend to result in reactionary positions. Doing something about something seems to be right. Again we submit, if we do not know why we do what we do, at best, we do it poorly or we do not even know when it is done.

Advocates of the various educational camps discussed in this monograph use language in an attempt to homogenize social reality and to eliminate disparate perceptions. Edelman (1973) establishes that language used by these educators tends to establish their reality and subtly justify their actions. This function is not unique to any one of the educational philosophic camps.

Declared positions relative to the purposes of of schooling must opt for one logically coherent

65

philosophy of education. As Roberts (1976, p. 321) succinctly states, "It is impossible to practice the ideas of Skinner and Chomsky simultaneously." In spite of good intentions educators cannot easily make congruent that which is incongruent.

Critics of schools generally assume one of two positions: "(1) they charge that the school lacks rigor, clarity of purpose, efficiency and a prudent economy, or (2) schools are a monolithic bureaucracy, preoccupied with convenience and tradition, depersonalized and uninterested in each child's individuality and removed from the realities of children's life environment" (Rubin, 1969, p. 4).

Seemingly, well-intentioned proponents of differing positions are more concerned with political rhetoric than with what is best for children and society. We would suggest that theory-practice congruency becomes a worthy goal of vocal proponents of the diverse camps in an attempt to provide children with an honest and good schooling experience.

It seems safe to establish that proponents of various philosophic camps are more concerned with finding better ways of doing what they are already doing than with raising questions as to why it is that they do what they do. Educational issues are a consequence of diverse conceptualizations of reality and values.

In the development of this monograph we did not intend to endorse a particular set of values. We did intend to suggest that those who make educational decisions might well afford to spend time and effort examining the philosophic roots of critical educational issues and problems. We strongly recommend that a focus be placed on developing and understanding basic systems of philosophy, as well as understanding linear relationships between educational points of view and day to day school methods, procedures, and methodology. We hoped the result of this effort would be that educators demonstrate a high level of sophistication in becoming more sensitive and aware of hidden or salient biases involved in recommendations and/or pressure to subscribe to current fads and trends in education. That was the purpose of this monograph.

References

Bailey, William. "A Case Study: Performance Evaluation at Concord Senior High School," Degrading the Grading Myths: A Primer of Alternatives to Grades and Marks. Sidney Simon and James Bellanca, eds., Washington, D.C.: Association for Supervision and Curriculum Development, 1976.

Bates, Marilyn M. and Clarence D. Johnson. Group Leadership. Denver, Colorado: Love Publishing Company, 1972.

Bellanca, James and Howard Kirschenbaum. "An Overview of Grading Alternatives," in Degrading the Grading Myths: A Primer of Alternatives to Grades and Marks. Sidney Simon and James Bellanca, eds., Washington, D.C.: Association for Supervision and Curriculum Development, 1976.

Berman, Louise. New Priorities in the Curriculum. Columbus, Ohio: Charles E. Merrill, 1967.

Berne, Eric. Games People Play. New York: Grove Press, Inc., 1964.

Bigge, Morris L. Learning Theories for Teachers. New York: Harper and Row Publishers, 1964.

Bloom Benjamin. "Learning for Mastery," Evaluation Comment of the University of California at Los Angeles, Center for the Study of Evaluation of Instructional Programs, Vol. 1, May 1968.

Brodinsky, Ben. "Back to the Basics: The Movement and Its Meaning," Phi Delta Kappan, 58:522-27, March 1977.

Bruner, Jerome S. The Process of Education. Cambridge: Harvard University Press, 1960.

_____, in Bruner, J. S., et.al., Contemporary Approaches to Cognition. Cambridge: Harvard University Press, 1957.

Combs, Arthur W. and Donald Snygg. Individual Behavior. New York: Harper and Row, 1959.

Curwin, Richard. "In Conclusion: Dispelling the
    Grading Myths," in Degrading the Grading Myths:
    A Primer of Alternative to Grades and Marks.
    Sydney Simon and James Bellanca, eds., Washing-
    ton, D.C.: Association for Supervision and
    Curriculum Development, 1976.

Daniels, J. C. "Effects of Streaming in the Primary
    School: A Comparison of Streamed and Unstreamed
    Schools," British Journal of Education Psychol-
    ogy, 31:119-27, 1961.

Dawson, Richard G. "A Conceptual Framework to Assess
    the Degree of Philosophical Harmony Within the
    Elementary School," Unpublished Doctoral Disser-
    tation, Oklahoma State University, Stillwater,
    1976.

Deci, E. L. "Changes in Intrinsic Motivation as a
    Function of Negative Feedback and Threats," ERIC
    Reports, ED 063 558. New York: Rochester Uni-
    versity, 1972a.

_____. "Intrinsic Motivation, Extrinsic Reinforce-
    ment and Inequity," Journal of Personality and
    Social Psychology, 22:113-29, 1972b.

Dimick, Kenneth M. and Vaughn E. Huff. Child Coun-
    seling. Dubuque, Iowa: William C. Brown, 1970.

Dobson, Judith E. and Russell L. Dobson. "School-
    Community Involvement: A Human Interactive
    Approach." Paper read at the American Personnel
    and Guidance Association Convention, St. Louis,
    Missouri, April 14, 1981.

Dobson, Russell L. and Judith E. Dobson. "Parental
    and Community Involvement in Education and
    Teacher Education," ERIC SP 008 742. Washington,
    D.C.: ERIC Clearinghouse on Teacher Education,
    1975.

Ebel, Robert. "What Are Schools For," Phi Delta
    Kappan, 54:3-7, September 1972.

Edelman, Murray. "The Political Language of the
    Helping Professions." Madison: University of
    Wisconsin, 1973. (Mimeographed.)

Eisner, Elliott. "The Curriculum Field Today: Where We Are, Where We Were." Paper read at the Society for Professors of Curriculum. Houston, Texas, March 1977.

Evans, Francis. "What Research Says About Grading," in Degrading the Grading Myths: A Primer of Alternatives to Grades and Marks. Sidney Simon and James Bellanca, eds., Washington, D.C.: Association for Supervision and Curriculum Development, 1976.

Farr, Roger and Jill E. Olshavsky. "Is Minimum Competency Testing the Appropriate Solution to the SAT Decline?" Phi Delta Kappan, 61:528-30, April 1980.

Frazier, Alexander. "Do We Really Want Better Teaching?" Educational Leadership, 34:138-42, November 1976.

Ford, Donald and Hugh Urban. Systems of Psychotherapy: A Comparative Study. New York: John Wiley and Sons, 1963.

Garbarino, J. "The Impact of Anticipated Reward Upon Cross-age Tutoring," Journal of Personality and Social Psychology, 32:421-28, 1975.

Goble, Frank. The Third Force. New York: Grossman Publishers, 1970.

Goldensen, Robert M. The Encyclopedia of Human Behavior. New York: Dell Publishing Company, 1975.

Goodlad, John. "Meeting Children Where They Are," Saturday Review, 48:57-59, March 20, 1965.

Green Maxine. Existential Encounters for Teachers. New York: Random House, 1967.

Johnson, Mauritz. "Definitions and Models in Curriculum Theory," Educational Theory, 17:122-28, April 1967.

Johnson, P. and R. Johnson. Learning Together and Alone: Cooperation, Competition, and Individualization. Englewood Cliffs, New Jersey: Prentice-Hall, 1975.

Kneller, George F. Introduction to the Philosophy
of Education. New York: John Wiley and Sons,
Inc., 1965.

Leonard, George. Education and Ecstacy. New York:
Delacorte Press, 1968.

Lepper, M. R. and Green, D. "On Understanding
'Overjustification': A Reply to Reiss and
Suskinsky," Journal of Personality and Social
Psychology, 33:25-35, 1976.

MacDonald, James. "A Curriculum Rationale," Contemporary Thought on Public School Curriculum,
Edmond Short and George Marconnit, editors.
Dubuque, Iowa: William C. Brown Co. Publishers,
1968.

_____. "Looking Toward the Future in Curriculum,"
Paper read at the Society for Professors of
Curriculum, Houston, Texas, March 1977.

MacDonald, James, Bernice Wolfson and Esther Zaret.
Reschooling Society: A Conceptual Model.
Washington, D.C.: Association for Supervision
and Curriculum Development, 1973.

Marshall, John. The Teacher and His Philosophy.
Lincoln, Nebraska: Professional Educators Pub-
lication, Inc., 1973.

Marler, Charles D. Philosophy and Schools. Boston:
Allyn and Bacon, Inc., 1975.

Maslow, Abraham H. Motivation and Personality.
Second edition. New York: Harper and Row, 1959.

May, Rollo. Love and Will. New York: W. W. Norton
and Company, Inc., 1969.

Morris, Van Cleve. Philosophy and the American
School. Boston: Houghton Mifflin Company, 1961.

National Elementary School Principals. Elementary
School Organization: Purposes, Patterns, Per-
spectives. Washington, D.C.: National Education
Association, 1961.

Patterson, C. H. Humanistic Education. Englewood
Cliffs, New Jersey: Prentice-Hall, Inc., 1973.

Piaget, Jean. The Psychology of the Child. Translated by Helen Weaver. New York: Basic Books, 1969.

Pipho, Chris (ed.). "Minimal Competency Testing," Phi Delta Kappan, 59:585-625, May 1978.

Purdom, Daniel. Exploring the Nongraded School. Dayton, Ohio: Institute for Development of Educational Activities, Inc., 1970.

Roberts, Joan. "Freedom, the Child, the Teacher: A Gap Between Ideas and Actions," Theory into Practice, 15:319-325, December 1976.

Rogers, Carl. "The Necessary and Sufficient Conditions of Therapeutic Personality Change," Journal of Consulting Psychology, 21:95-103, 1957.

_____. On Becoming a Person. Boston: Houghton Mifflin, 1961.

_____. On Personal Power. New York: Delacorte Press, 1977.

Rogers, Vincent and Joan Baron. "Declining Scores: A Humanistic Explanation," Phi Delta Kappan, 58:311-13, December 1976.

Rosenthal, Robert and Lenore Jacobson. Pygmalion in the Classroom: Teacher Expectations and Pupils' Intellectual Development. New York: Holt, Rinehart and Winston, Inc., 1968.

Rubin, Louis. "The Object of Schooling: An Evolutionary View," in Life Skills in School and Society, Louis Rubin editor, Washington, D.C.: Association of Supervision and Curriculum Development, 1969.

Samples, Robert and Robert Wohlford. Opening. Reading, Massachusetts: Addison-Wesley Publishing Co., 1973.

Sargent, S. Stansfeld and Kenneth Stafford. Basic Teachings of the Great Psychologists. Garden City, N.Y.: Doubleday and Company, Inc., 1965.

Simon, Sidney. "An Overview in Degrading the Grading
    Myths: A Primer of Alternatives to Grades and
    Marks. Sidney Simon and James Bellanca, editors.
    Washington, D.C.: Association of Supervision and
    Curriculum Development, 1977.

Sloan, Fred. "Elementary School Organization."
    Norman: University of Oklahoma, 1964. (Mimeo-
    graphed.)

Smith, B. Othaniel, William Stanley and J. Harlan
    Shores. Fundamentals of Curriculum Development.
    Chicago: Harcourt, Brace and World, Inc., 1957.

Sulzer, Beth and G. Roy Mayer. Behavior Modification
    Procedures for School Personnel. Hinsdale,
    Illinois: The Dryden Press, Inc., 1972.

Thorndike, Edward L. Selected Writings from a Connec-
    tionist's Psychology. Appleton-Century-Crofts,
    1949.

_____. Educational Psychology. Teachers College,
    Columbia, University, 1913.

_____. Education. MacMillan, 1912.

Turlington, Ralph D. "Good News From Florida: Our
    Minimum Competency Program is Working," Phi Delta
    Kappan, 60:649-51, May 1979.

Van Hoven, J. B. "Reporting Pupil Progress: A Broad
    Rationale for New Practices," Phi Delta Kappan,
    53:365-66, February 1972.

Wadsworth, Barry J. Piaget's Theory of Cognitive
    Development. New York: David McKay, Inc., 1971.

Wingo, G. Max. Philosophies of Education: An Intro-
    duction. Lexington, Massachusetts: D. C. Heath
    and Company, 1974.

SUBJECT INDEX